THE G.I. SERIES

An unidentified company grade officer of the First U.S. Cavalry displays the numeral '1' in silver below his officer's hat insignia in keeping with the directive for cavalry officers set forth in General Orders No. 7, Adjutant General's Office, 24 June 1858. He retains the dark blue woollen trousers that were regulation until 16 December 1861. The epaulettes are gold, the sash crimson silk. The gauntlets, although not called for in regulations, were a common accessory for cavalrymen, particularly officers.

THE G. I. SERIES

THE ILLUSTRATED HISTORY OF THE AMERICAN SOLDIER, HIS UNIFORM AND HIS EQUIPMENT

Billy Yank
The Uniform of the Union Army
1861–1865

Michael J. McAfee and John P. Langellier

CHELSEA HOUSE PUBLISHERS
PHILADELPHIA

Library of Congress Cataloging-in-Publication Data
McAfee, Michael J.
Billy Yank: the uniform of the Union Army, 1861–1865 / Michael J. McAfee, John P. Langellier.
     p.   cm.—(GI series)
Originally published: London : Greenhill Books; Mechanicsburg, Pa., USA: Stackpole Books, © 1996, in series: The G.I. series; 4
Includes index.
Summary: Describes the uniforms worn by members of the Union Army during the Civil War.
ISBN 0-7910-5368-7 (hc.)
1. United States. Army—Uniforms—History—
19th century.   2. United States—History—Civil War, 1861–1865. [1. United States. Army—Uniforms—History.   2. United States—History—Civil War, 1861–1865.]   I. Langellier, J. Philip.   II. Title.
UC483.M3   1999
355.1'4'097309034—dc21   99-21377
                                                        CIP

ACKNOWLEDGEMENTS

All black and white illustrations in this volume are property of Michael J. McAfee. Colour images were made possible through the assistance of Michael Moss and David Meschutt, of the West Point Museum, Kevin Mulroy, Autry Museum of Western Heritage, and photographer Susan Einstein. This book is dedicated to the memory of Frederick P. Todd.

ABBREVIATIONS

AMWH	Autry Museum of Western Heritage
BL	Bancroft Library, Berkeley, CA
FAM	Frontier Army Museum, Fort Leavenworth, KS
FDNHS	Fort Davis National Historic Site
FLNHS	Fort Laramie National Historic Site
LBNB	Little Bighorn National Battlefield
LC	Library of Congress
NARS	National Archives Records Service
KSHS	Kansas State Historical Society, Topeka
RBM	Reno Battlefield Museum, Garryowen, MT
SI	Smithsonian Institution, Museum of American History
USAMHI	US Army Military History Institute, Carlisle Barracks, PA
UKL	Pennell Collection, Kansas Collections, University of Kansas Libraries, Lawrence
USCM	US Cavalry Museum, Fort Riley, KS
WSM	Wyoming State Museum, Cheyenne

Designed and edited by DAG Publications Ltd
Designed by David Gibbons
Layout by Anthony A. Evans
Printed in Hong Kong

BILLY YANK:
THE UNIFORM OF THE UNION ARMY, 1861–1865

Abraham Lincoln's victory in the presidential election of 1860 triggered a reaction among seven southern states. By February 1861 all seven asserted their sovereignty and declared their departure from the Union. The breakaways then set about the establishment of a provisional government, calling themselves the Confederate States of America. Not long afterwards they started to seize federal property, including military posts. Soon, only Fortress Monroe in Virginia, Fort Pickens in Florida, and Fort Sumter in South Carolina continued to fly the U.S. flag. Then, on 12 April 1861 artillery fire shattered the strained peace as Confederate batteries in Charleston Harbor blasted away against the brick bastion that stood as a symbol of federal authority.

Inside its casemates, Major Robert Anderson and his command responded with their own barrages. The duel proved short lived. By 14 April Anderson and his ninety men were forced to surrender Fort Sumter. The American Civil War had begun.

In response to these opening salvos, Lincoln called upon the governors of loyal states to furnish some 75,000 volunteers to squash the secessionists. This body of men was to serve for three months and provide a sizeable reinforcement to the small Regular Army of approximately 16,000 officers and men which Lincoln had at his disposal when he came to office. In addition, the president gained congressional authority to expand the regulars by one field artillery regiment, another of cavalry, and eight of infantry (ultimately a ninth was included), as well as muster into service another forty regiments of U.S. Volunteers comprising some 42,000 fighting men. On paper all this appeared adequate to the task at hand, a short conflict being expected.

In reality those who responded early to the call to arms ultimately proved insufficient in numbers, and at best represented a mixed lot when it came to trained soldiers led by competent officers. And they rallied to the Union cause in a variety of outfits that resulted in anything but uniformity in the early part of the conflict. A range of colors and cuts made it difficult to determine which side some of these units belonged to, and resulted in confusion during some of the opening engagements. Northern troops appearing in gray sometimes were mistaken for Southern forces.

In other instances the uniforms were gaudy and impracticable – fine for parades by militia but not suited to combat. Tall bearskins, coatees with considerable trim, and outfits which had been adopted more out of patriotic fervor rather than practical considerations proliferated. In a number of instances national origins took precedence over providing a readily identifiable connection with the North. There were Irish, Scots, Italian, and French units whose members often hailed from those countries or traced their ancestry to them. In a number of instances they chose to adopt a dress that reflected these specific European roots. Then there were those who had no connection to Europe *per se* but were smitten by foreign martial fashion – most notably by the Zouaves, a Franco-Algerian military formation which roused considerable interest in the United States not long after the Crimean War. Their uniform was even issued to some African American units after blacks entered the federal ranks halfway through the war.

Still other companies and regiments joined in haste with little concern for their kit. There were those who arrived for duty in civilian garb, with only accouterments and weapons to mark them as a military organization.

These men had to be clothed, as ultimately did hundreds of thousands more as the conflict escalated from what many thought would be a short affair to a prolonged, bloody series of engagements over four desperate years. At the start the Confederates held a military advantage, primarily because the Union troops had to go on the offensive and invade the enemy's territory in order, as one historian phrased it, to 'subdue a valorous people zealously fighting for what it considered to be its liberty, its honor, its very existence'. This proved a formidable task. Indeed, during the opening months of the war Southern strategy prevailed. The idea simply was to wait. Union soldiers would have to come to them, and that was just what happened.

In turn, Northern objectives broadened, not only to capture Richmond, but also, as historian T. Harry Williams summarized: 'To smash the army defending the capital, to grasp the line of the Mississippi River, thus splitting the Confederacy into two parts; and after the second objective had been achieved, to seize Chattanooga on the Tennessee River line, thereby securing a base from which to launch an offensive to divide the Confederacy again.'

These ambitious goals proved costly for both sides. The North, even with its industrial superiority, found it not only difficult to clothe its armies, but also to supply them with all the required *matériel* to prosecute the war. Weapons sometimes even had to be procured abroad to arm the growing ranks of the Union. This led to high costs, especially when various agents of the government ended up bidding against one another for foreign ordnance, thereby inflating already high prices.

The feeding of what was to become one of the largest armies ever fielded to that time likewise was a major task. While the canning process had become practical by this period and experiments in the preservation of foodstuffs were being undertaken, the troops still required considerable quantities of 'fresh' food – the term being relative in many instances. Pork, or 'fatback' as it was known, could be old and rancid as could beef rations. These were staples to be eaten with hard bread, a kind of thick cracker also referred to as hard crackers or hardtack. The troops would soak these items in fat, crush them, or in other ways attempt to make them more digestible if not more palatable. Coffee was another major ingredient in the monotonous field fare, which also was far from healthy. Many men suffered from lack of proper diet, bad drinking water, and similar problems. In fact, many fell ill to a range of maladies from dysentery to measles and chicken pox. Some died. Many more were out of action from diseases that took a higher toll than those struck down by the enemy.

Medical care varied greatly, but generally was inadequate given the enormous problems confronting the medicos and also given the state of the medical arts of the era. A man might survive a Rebel round only to die of shock, loss of blood, or complications from surgery, most notably gangrene.

Other problems faced the Yankees as well, most notably a lack of leadership when it came to the high command. Lincoln began his search for a commander who could stand up to the Confederates, and settled for Major General George B. McClellan as one of many unsuccessful generals the president placed in charge.

Early the next year activities increased, but not under McClellan. Instead, the action shifted to the West where, in January, Brigadier General George Thomas gained one of the first significant federal victories over the South at Mill Springs, Kentucky. During the following month, another Yankee rising star in the western theater, Ulysses S. Grant, also handed the Rebels a defeat by capturing Fort Henry on the Tennessee and Fort Donelson on the Cumberland. The determined Grant repeated his success, although only after reversing the initial Confederate onslaught at Shiloh, Tennessee, in April.

April likewise saw McClellan finally move his army from Washington to Yorktown, Virginia, a proposed springboard for a drive to Richmond. A number of engagements followed, with the Army of North Virginia, under Robert E. Lee, finally sending McClellan and his Army of the Potomac northward by water. The Second Battle of Bull Run and Antietam were the unfortunate results, with Lee emerging as victor in both cases. He ended the year by besting Major General Ambrose Burnside at Fredericksburg, Virginia.

It was the West again that offered the Union better news by 1863. After a long siege, a determined Grant captured Vicksburg, thereby opening the Mississippi River to the Gulf of Mexico. Another Northern general in the West, William Rosecrans, emulated Grant by taking Chattanooga, only to suffer a reversal at Chickamauga.

The South likewise prevailed in May 1863 at Chancellorsville with Lee's 57,000 men against 134,000, under Joseph Hooker. On 1 May the Union leader had succeeded in deploying almost half his army across the Rappahannock near Chancellorsville, Virginia, even as another 25,000 Billy Yanks were on their way to join the massive advance. It appeared as if Lincoln had found someone who knew how to drive the war into enemy territory. That assumption disappeared when Stonewall Jackson reached the scene with 30,000 Johnny Rebs, and joined their comrades, another 16,000 in number, who had already entrenched themselves and were awaiting Hooker.

Ever daring, Jackson combined his forces, and rather than dig in gave the word to take the offensive. The two sides soon converged with the opening contact causing confusion for Hooker. In the process he reversed his tactics and went on the defensive, his troops taking up positions around the town to meet Jackson's onslaught and in the process 'were surprised, outnumbered, outflanked, and unsupported'. So the Yankees fell back with only limited resistance.

By 3 May the Confederates had pressed the advantage. Hooker himself was wounded, but fared better than Jackson, who the night before had been shot when some of his own men took him for an enemy in the dark and fired upon him. Jackson died days later from complications after a Confederate surgeon amputated.

Nearly two months later it appeared as if the Confederates might gain another victory when Lee's army, now organized into three equal corps of three divisions each, set course for an invasion of Union territory. At the head of 155,000 men, Lee moved toward the Potomac, crossed, and by late June two of his corps were nearing Chambersburg, Pennsylvania. The Rebels were squarely in the Yankees' backyard.

In the process, Lee lost contact with his cavalry, thereby being deprived of a valuable source of intelligence about his adversary, Hooker. In the meantime Hooker had taken up positions to block an attack on Washington, after which he asked to be relieved of his command. This left his replacement, George Meade, with the problem of determining what move the Army of the Potomac must make next.

On 1 July the enemy dictated Meade's course. Although neither he nor Lee wanted to give battle that day, circumstances took the situation out of their hands. Elements of the Union I Corps approached Gettysburg, Pennsylvania from the south-east. Throughout 3 July the two sides engaged furiously, but Gettysburg would prove to be 'the high-water mark' of the Confederacy, ending in a confused mass with many dead, wounded, and captured. Leaving behind nineteen regimental colors, the Southern survivors returned to their lines and regrouped under Lee to return to the South.

Gettysburg and Vicksburg represented key battles for the North, allowing Lincoln's armies to consider other strategic options, most notably Chattanooga, a railroad hub and corridor for the Yankees to strike deeper into Rebel territory. Confederate General Braxton Bragg meant to deprive the Union's commander, William Rosecrans, of this objective. Both sides marched in September, the South originally being on the defensive, and met at Chickamauga. As a result, Rosecrans' troops had fallen back by the end of the month to Chattanooga where they prepared for a siege.

Given this state of affairs, Lincoln looked to another leader to solve Rosecrans' predicament. He called upon Grant to resume the offensive. His faith was not misplaced. The cigar-chomping general launched his troops against Bragg in November and soon was in pursuit of a fleeing enemy. It was only a matter of time before the Confederacy would collapse.

Events of 1864 further contributed to the Union's momentum, one of the key ingredients being Grant's promotion to commander of all the federal forces in both the eastern and western theaters. Grant now sought to throw his military might against the opposition in a concerted effort, sending the Army of the Potomac, the Army of the James, and the XI Corps against Lee. Grant's right hand in the West, William Sherman, was to strike into the interior of the Confederacy with as deep and lethal a thrust as possible. By early May 1864 the time to implement this plan had come.

Sherman, with the tenacity of a bulldog, drove into the South. Although he faced a staunch foe in General Joseph Johnston, he would not yield. Throughout August Sherman's march pressed toward Atlanta, a critical industrial center. By the beginning of September his men took the city. From there he boldly proposed to continue his advance all the way to the Atlantic, living off the land *en route* and destroying everything in his wake. It was total war.

Even as Sherman was bringing the mailed fist to the Confederate interior, his commanding officer, Grant, looked toward Richmond. In May the Army of the Potomac led off. The invading columns would again clash with the Army of Northern Virginia at, for example, the Battle of the Wilderness, and Yellow Tavern where the Confederacy's dashing cavalier, J. E. B. Stuart, was struck down. In the wake of Yellow Tavern, the Army of Northern Virginia's offensive cavalry capabilities had been brought to a shadow of their former effectiveness.

While Sheridan was wreaking havoc on horseback, Grant made a general attack against both the east and west faces of Lee's lines at Spotsylvania, beginning on 10 May. The fighting on the west proved the fiercest, and Grant gradually turned his concentration on the east, Lee's right flank, where the Yankees hoped to envelop the Rebels.

Lee dug in again, and avoided entrapment. As one historian put it, this 'side-slipping process was continued, from position to position, until Lee came out of the defenses of Richmond, his right on the Chickahominy and his left at Cold Harbor ...' Although he had been pushed back to the Confederate capital, Lee skilfully denied Grant success, at the cost of some 25,000 to 30,000 casualties from his army, while Grant had sustained 55,000 to 60,000 dead, wounded, or captured during the bloody campaign. The Northern press began to refer to Grant as a butcher, but this charge did not dissuade him from his unrelenting course to draw Lee into open confrontation.

With that intent Grant withdrew from the vicinity of Richmond on 12 June. He now set his sights on Petersburg, with an attack on the fifteenth, but the outcome did not go as planned and a siege of Petersburg ensued.

Lee wanted to derail the Union efforts. To this end he once more decided to make a run at Washington in the belief that Grant would have to transfer forces to the north as a precaution against the Southern raiders. General Jubal Early carried out Lee's plan but with little effect. Grant sent only a token number from his army, while Lincoln recommended that a concerted effort be made to crush Early. Responding to the president, Grant unleashed Sheridan, whose superior force engaged and defeated Early in September and October at Winchester, Fisher's Hill, and Cedar Creek respectively.

Early withdrew even as Grant continued to press Petersburg, and Sherman kept driving on towards Savannah, Georgia, which fell in late December. Sherman then moved on toward the Army of the Potomac, all the while destroying enemy crops, communications, and other resources that sustained the Southern war effort. Then, in January 1865, he swung north. Additional Union troops left Tennessee to join Grant. Sheridan pulled out of the Shenandoah with further reinforcements for the final push to topple the Confederacy.

With superior numbers in place and having a number of veteran Billy Yanks in the ranks, the Union at last was in a position to force Lee from Petersburg and Richmond. Lee's reserves being exhausted, on 9 April 1865 he had no choice but to surrender his army at Appomattox. The time had come to bind up old wounds, and 'with malice toward none,' for a nation which had been torn asunder by civil war to reunite.

FOR FURTHER READING

Boatner, Mark III. *The Civil War Dictionary*. New York, David McCay Company, Inc., 1959

Delano, Marfé Ferguson, and Mallen, Barbara C. *Echoes of Glory: Arms and Equipment of the Union*. Alexandria, Va, Time-Life Books, 1991

Schuyler, Hartley and Graham. *Illustrated Catalog of Civil War Military Goods, Union Weapons, Uniform Accessories and Other Equipment*. New York, Dover Publications, Inc., 1985

Todd, Frederick P. *American Military Equipage 1851-1872*. 3 vols. Providence, RI, and Westbrook, Ct, Company of Military Historians, 1974-8.

Wiley, Bell I. (ed.). *The Image of War 1861-1865*. 5 vols. Gettysburg, The National Historical Society, 1981

Above: When the Civil War began in 1861 the regulation trousers were of dark blue wool, although later that year general orders changed the color to sky-blue for officers and enlisted men alike. In this lithograph the earlier color of trousers is seen, worn by a sergeant of engineers in the background and two officers on the left of Winfield Scott, the general commanding the U.S. Army at the outbreak of the war. Scott wears his custom-designed uniform, a privilege extended to all general officers. (Autry Museum of Western Heritage)

Left: Henry Bacon's *Reveille on a Winter Morning* provides many details about uniforms. The 1851-pattern overcoat issued to infantry and other dismounted troops in the Union Army particularly is prominent. This sky-blue wool kersey garment was one of the few items available to federal soldiers for protection against inclement weather. (West Point Museum, U.S. Academy, West Point, New York)

Below: W. Winner's *Union Assault on Confederate Works* shows both the regulation forage cap and non-regulation slouch hats worn by these blue-clad troops in their four-button sack coats, one of the most common of the outer garments worn by the Yankees during the Civil War. (West Point Museum)

Below: Major General George B. McClellan wears the 1851-pattern general officer's cloak coat with optional cape, the black silk braid on his sleeve indicating rank. Underneath, his dark blue woollen double-breasted frock coat has three sets of three buttons as a further means to indicate that he is a major general. (West Point Museum)

Above: Philip Sheridan wears the frock coat of a major general with its black velvet collar and cuffs and shoulder-straps with two silver stars on a black background bordered by gold embroidery. His general officer's gold hat cords fly off to the side revealing their acorn tips. The hat and gauntlets are non-regulation but typical of the numerous items privately purchased by officers and enlisted men alike. (West Point Museum)

Above: Paul E. Harney's painting of cavalry troopers wearing the distinctive short jacket which bore twelve buttons down the front and which was trimmed in yellow worsted lace for enlisted men as they relax on patrol. The officer riding by wears his crimson sash around his waist. (West Point Museum)

Right: A painting by James Walker depicts mounted Union officers on Missionary Ridge. A company grade officer (on the right side) is indicated by his single-breasted dark blue woollen frock coat. (West Point Museum)

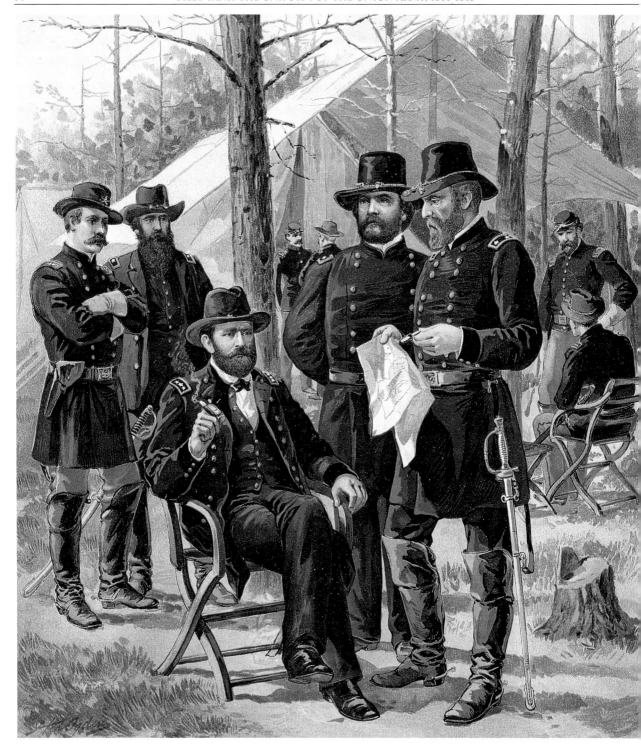

Above: U. S. Grant as a lieutenant general (indicated by three stars on dark blue or black-backed shoulder-straps) looks less soldierly than some of his subordinates, who surround him in this illustration by H. A. Ogden. The practical, no-nonsense look was associated with both Grant and the troops he led in the Western theater of operations. As the war continued, function took precedence over form in many ways. (Autry Museum of Western Heritage)

Above: Standing in the center of this composition, wearing a civilian-style slouch hat, is a major general (indicated by the nine buttons placed in sets of three on his double-breasted frock coat). He is talking to a company grade officer of light artillery, distinguished by the unique cap with scarlet horsetail plume. Most of the remainder of the officers and enlisted men are wearing the 1858-pattern hat, looped on the right for officers and mounted troops and on the left for all other ranks. By 1861, sky-blue trousers with a scarlet, yellow, or dark blue welt were worn by artillery, cavalry, and infantry officers respectively; plain dark blue trousers were prescribed for generals and staff officers. All enlisted men wore sky-blue trousers – plain for privates, with a ½-inch leg stripe for corporals, and a 1½-inch stripe for sergeants, all in branch of service colors. The dress uniforms depicted here, while regulation from 1861 until the end of 1872, were seldom seen except in Washington, DC, at least during the Civil War. (Autry Museum of Western Heritage)

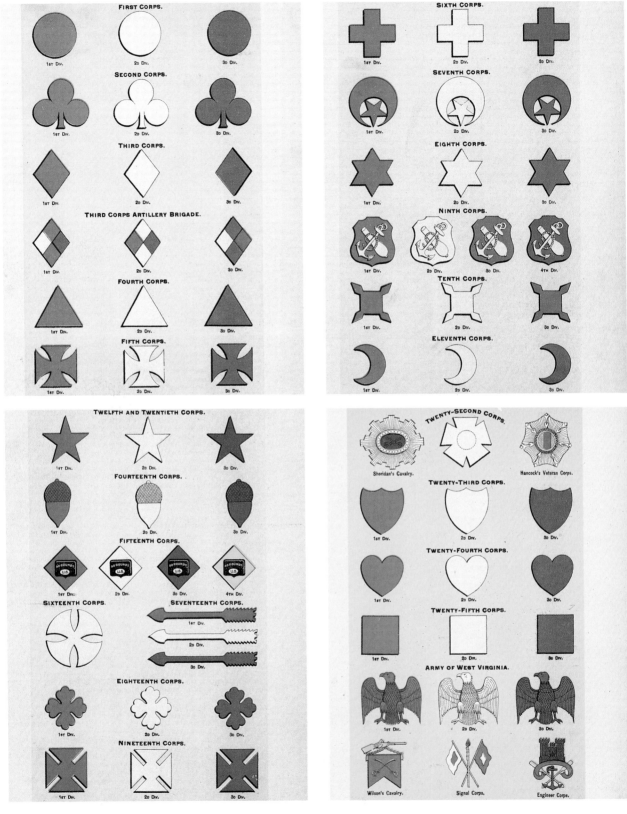

Starting in June 1862, in Philip Kearny's division, Union commanders gradually adopted badges to designate corps and divisions. They were worn on caps, coats, and other garments. Some were mere patches of cloth cut in geometric shapes, other more elaborate designs were made of metal.

By the end of the war numerous types existed and the practice had been more or less regulated into a rational system as seen in these illustrations. (Michael McAfee Collection)

Right: Although the option of wearing the *chapeau de bras* existed from the very beginning of the war, most field grade officers chose to wear the 1858-pattern hat with three ostrich feathers, as seen here worn by this infantry officer who posed for the portrait in about 1861. He is wearing the dark blue woollen trousers with light blue welt. The sword is a non-regulation private purchase. Note that the hat is looped up on the right side as per General Orders No. 4, Adjutant General's Office, 26 February 1861.

Left: The dark blue woollen double-breasted frock coat with seven gilt buttons in each row was regulation for U.S. Army field grade officers (majors and colonels). It is seen here worn by Colonel Erasmus Keyes, Eleventh U.S. Infantry in 1861; his dark blue trousers have the ⅛-inch light blue welt. He is holding what seems to be the so-called 'French chapeau', a head-dress made available on an optional basis for generals and field grade officers in 1860.

Right: In 1861, Brigadier General Scott Negley of the Eighteen Division of the Pennsylvania Militia had his own ideas as to what constituted a well-dressed leader of men – they reflected European rather than American fashion.

Left: In the first year of the war the Virginian Winfield Scott remained loyal to the Union, and stoically sat for the camera wearing his special dark blue frock coat of his own design with gold embroidered oak leaves on the cuffs and turn-down collar, the same motif being carried over to his sword belt which has a custom interlocking circular gilt buckle bearing the motif 'U.S.' in the center. The wide sash was buff and the trousers dark blue.

Above: Brigadier General O. M. Mitchel remained more faithful to regulations than Scott and Negley, his blue woollen double-breasted frock coat exhibiting the correctly spaced four pairs of general staff buttons, a total of eight in each row. The plain black velvet cuffs and collar, the red sword belt with three gold embroidered stripes, and the buff silk sash are likewise 'by the book'. He is wearing brigadier general's shoulder-straps with outer edges of gold embroidery around a black center, bearing a single silver star on each strap. He is holding a forage cap with the silver 'U.S.' within a gold embroidered wreath.

Above: Major General J. A. Dix also closely approximated the regulations when it came to his double-breasted frock coat with nine buttons per row grouped in sets of three. He has chosen to wear epaulettes rather than shoulder-straps, both insignia of rank being correct depending on the order of dress required. His belt, however, is a plain black leather one with a 'U.S.' buckle, neither feature being regulation.

Below: The distinctive garb for hospital stewards evolved between 1857 and 1861. In the former year the basic outfit finally was defined as a single-breasted nine-button frock coat with crimson piping around the collar and at each cuff, and matching trousers of dark blue wool. A green half-chevron with yellow borders and a yellow silk thread embroidered caduceus was placed in the center of the device and these were worn at downward angles above the elbow. As of General Orders No. 108, Headquarters of the U.S. Army, 16 December 1861, sky-blue trousers with a worsted 1½-inch crimson stripe down the outer seams were to replace the dark blue trousers. A red worsted sash was wrapped twice around the waist and tied at the left (as prescribed for all NCOs from first sergeant or orderly sergeant and above). This individual is wearing a low-crowned *chasseur*'s forage cap which bears an officer's-style small embroidered gold wreath with silver script 'U.S.' instead of the larger metallic insignia called for by regulations. A white dress collar is also evident.

Below: The forage cap, four-button sack, and sky-blue kersey trousers are typical of regulars after December 1861, when the lighter shade of trousers were re-adopted to replace dark blue versions issued prior to the outbreak of the war. The accouterments also are representative for Union infantrymen.

Right: New York, with the largest population in the United States, accordingly furnished a sizeable number of troops to the Union cause. With many soldiers to clothe, the diversity which existed among New York units typified the lack of uniformity found among the federal forces, particularly early in the war. Private George Miller, Twenty-fifth New York Volunteer Cavalry, wears an outfit no different from that issued to regulars before the war, and which had become widespread for all enlisted men by the time the war ended. The four-button sack coat and the forage cap (nicknamed the 'bummer's cap') are both dark; the kersey trousers are sky-blue.

Left: In 1861, a sergeant of the Second Regiment New York State Militia (later to become the Eighty-second New York Volunteers) stands proudly in an elaborate triple-breasted frock coat which resembled the type worn by the Seventy-first New York, although the broad white stripe on his trousers and the numeral in his hat differentiated the two organisations. Epaulettes with gilt crescents and chevrons, which may be of bullion lace, embellish the coat.

Right: Despite the popular notion that the North always wore blue, many Union units started the war in gray, such as the Seventh New York State Militia. The facings were black on the shoulder loops, cuffs and collar of the fatigue uniform.

Above: The Seventh New York's dress uniform featured gray trousers, a gray coatee with black trim, and a shako with a large metal plate surmounted by a tall pompon. Only the trousers were retained for field use, the remainder of the parade kit being put aside.

Left: These Seventh New York State Militia NCOs forming a color guard exhibit the black lace chevrons worn by corporals and sergeants in this unit, presumably of worsted tape either applied directly to the sleeves points down or on backings of the same cloth as the uniform jacket.

Above: Officers of the Seventh New York retained the gray trousers, but instead of a plain black stripe along the outer seams they had a double row of gold lace over red, in keeping with the fact that this was an artillery unit. They also wore the dark blue woollen nine-button single-breasted frock coat, as Second Lieutenant Tuthill models in this 1861 picture. His plain shoulder-straps with scarlet centers indicate his rank, and the embroidered cap device his unit affiliation.

Left: This youthful member of the Blenker's First German Rifles wears a forage cap bearing the bugle device associated with that branch. His sack coat, with adjustable back pleats, has cuffs, collar, and shoulder loops trimmed in green, the traditional color for rifle units.

Below: Even within one regiment, uniformity was not always to be found, as indicated by these soldiers from the Eighth New York State Militia, or Washington Grays, who are encamped in July 1861 just prior to the 'First Battle of Bull Run'. Most of them are wearing plain, loose fitting gray shirts issued by the state to several regiments as an outer garment when coats were not available, although the man with the axe has the regimental fatigue jacket with shoulder loops, cuffs, and collar trimmed in black. Note also that the man with his bayonet fixed has full marching gear in place including a haversack, tin cup, and a blanket roll over his right shoulder which both Union and Confederate troops often favored over backpacks or knapsacks.

Right: Although blanket rolls might have been more practical, hard-framed European-style backpacks were issued to many units, including the Ninth New York State Militia. Dark blue trousers and a matching jacket trimmed in red and a dark blue forage cap with gilt braid were the standard fatigue outfit; the overcoat draped on the chair is of dark blue with red cuff tabs and a red lined cape. This member of the Ninth is a corporal as indicated by his red worsted chevrons with two stripes worn points down.

Far left: The insignia on the forage cap of this sergeant of the Thirteenth New York State Militia, Company 'B', gives an indication that he was not a member of the Seventh New York. Additionally, the Seventh wore black leg stripes on their trousers while this member of the Thirteenth does not.

Near left: The City of Brooklyn furnished the Fourteenth New York State Militia (later converted to the Eighty-fourth Volunteers) with blue jackets ornamented with ball buttons and red trim, together with red vests, caps, and trousers. Sky-blue trousers were worn for fatigue duty. This uniform was adopted in 1860 and drew upon French military style, but it was a hybrid adaptation rather than a copy.

Right: In part because of their resemblance to Rebel gunners, the Twenty-second New York abandoned their 'strawberry gray' uniform in 1863, in favor of a dark blue *chasseur*'s coat piped in light blue, as worn by this trio from the regiment in about 1864.

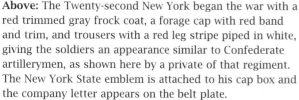

Above: The Twenty-second New York began the war with a red trimmed gray frock coat, a forage cap with red band and trim, and trousers with a red leg stripe piped in white, giving the soldiers an appearance similar to Confederate artillerymen, as shown here by a private of that regiment. The New York State emblem is attached to his cap box and the company letter appears on the belt plate.

Above right: In his state volunteer jacket of dark blue trimmed with bright blue on the shoulder-straps and collar, Private Gabriel Smith, Fifty-sixth New York Volunteer Infantry, is further distinguished by the Roman numeral X, for the unit's other designation, the Tenth Legion. The picture dates from 1861.

Right: A private of the Forty-second New York Volunteer Infantry wearing an 1858-pattern infantry frock with light blue trim on collar and cuffs and sky-blue kersey trousers. The only features distinguishing this from a regular army uniform are the brass numerals of his regiment on each side of the collar, and a bugle device which is smaller than the 1858-pattern adopted for the regular army hat, and – interestingly – is very similar to the pattern adopted in 1872 by the U.S. Army for infantry troops. Additionally, the forage cap is the *chasseur* style rather than the floppy 'bummer's.'

Below: White crossed belts formed another part of the Seventy-first New York's outfit as did chevrons of light blue for NCOs – seen on the sleeve of the corporal on the left of the photograph. The officer, a second lieutenant, has no welt let into the seams of his trousers, unlike the enlisted men who appear in this group portrait. The lieutenant is wearing a company grade nine-button frock coat, and his forage cap, which rests on a knapsack on the right of the picture, has an embroidered wreath with the numerals '71' in the center, whereas the other ranks have metal numerals on their caps.

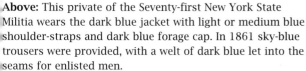

Above: This private of the Seventy-first New York State Militia wears the dark blue jacket with light or medium blue shoulder-straps and dark blue forage cap. In 1861 sky-blue trousers were provided, with a welt of dark blue let into the seams for enlisted men.

Above right: The 143rd New York Volunteer Infantry had Austrian rifled muskets in .54 or .55 caliber, with sword bayonets. Sergeant Austin Race of this regiment has the 'SNY' (State of New York) oval brass belt plate and the dark blue jacket with eight New York buttons and standing collar prescribed by a uniform board in that state in April 1861. This photograph was taken in the following year. Note the exterior pockets – a practical detail although against military fashion of the time.

Left: Cradling his Sharps Rifle, a private of Company 'A', 151st New York Volunteer Infantry, known as 'Bowen's Independent Rifles', has slung his canteen, which in this case probably was of the type covered in sky-blue cloth. The trim on his frock coat and his leg stripe possibly are green.

Opposite page, left: By mid war the state of New York had adopted a 'polka-skirted' uniform for its militiamen, a style that had been in vogue for some New York units previously. A private of the Twenty-ninth Regiment, National Guard in 1864 is wearing the new dark blue jacket with white piping. His cap pompon is red, white, and blue.

Opposite page, right: In 1862 and 1863 the Thirty-seventh Regiment New York National Guard graduated from wearing the U.S. Army frock coat and forage cap for infantry to the 1861 State of New York's plain dark blue fatigue jacket with sky-blue trousers, and then, in 1864, to yet a third outfit, consisting of a dark blue jacket and forage cap, both trimmed in red, and sky-blue trousers with a red welt. The numeral '37' appeared on the cap and breast plate for the cartridge box, over the shoulder-belt, and the company letter on the waist-belt plate.

Opposite page, left: From 1860 to 1861 the Fourth Battalion of Rifles of the Massachusetts Militia, although coming from a state that had a Revolutionary War history, eschewed the tricorn worn by some New England units in favor of a gray forage cap with red pompon and red lace trim. The coat was gray with red trim and red 'Russian' knots. Chevrons for NCOs likewise were red as shown here by Sergeant Sigourney Wales' coat. Gray trousers with a red welt completed the outfit, and the longarm was a M1841 rifle (Windsor) fitted with a saber bayonet.

Opposite page, right: Lieutenant Augustus Sampson of the Fourth Battalion of Rifles, Massachusetts Volunteer Militia appears in the 1860 to 1861 officer's uniform of that unit (which became the Thirteenth Volunteer Infantry Regiment). The feathers on his cap are red as is the band and the knots. The coat appears to be a darker shade of gray than the trousers; it may have been blue. The bugle on his hip reflects the light infantry nature of the regiment, which used bugles rather than drums for signalling orders.

Right: Captain William Thompson, who commanded a company of the Forty-third New York Volunteer Infantry, wears a short jacket with nine buttons rather than a company grade officer's frock coat. His dark blue vest and trousers give a monotone effect. The black campaign hat has officer's gold and black cords but no other insignia.

Above: Chaplains, like Edward Lord, 110th New York Volunteers, seen here in 1862, improvised their uniform because they were not obliged to follow the requirements set forth in General Orders No. 102, Adjutant General's Office, 25 November 1861, which stated: 'The uniforms for chaplains of the army will be plain frock coat with standing collar, and one row of nine black buttons; plain black pantaloons; black felt hat, or army forage cap without ornament.' Bible in hand, Lord has added a medical or pay department officer's sword to the basic uniform which, while it conforms to General Orders No. 102, has the addition of a general staff captain's shoulder-straps – a rough equivalent of his rank (chaplains were to receive the pay and allowances of a cavalry captain) – and a sash of an indeterminate color.

Above: A typical embroidered Arms of the United States side-piece for the 1858-pattern officer's hat is evident in this photograph of Colonel Lewis Campbell, Sixty-ninth Ohio Volunteer Infantry, taken in about 1861.

Right: Appearing very much in the garb of a regular, Surgeon Yorick Hurd, Forty-eighth Massachusetts Volunteer Infantry, only differs from his U.S. Army counterparts in that the buttons bear the state seal and the cap device is a silver embroidered script 'M.S.' rather than a 'U.S.'. The sword is the M1840 Medical Department's edged weapon.

Left: Captain Orlando Nims, who commanded a battery named after him, and which was raised as part of the state of Massachusetts's contribution to the Union, holds a forage cap with sloping visor popularly known today as the 'McDowell' pattern, so called because it was favored by Major General Irvin McDowell. For some reason he is shouldering a trumpet for this portrait. It was probably a 'prop', much loved by photographers of the time, but which can give rise to erroneous assumptions about accouterments and uniforms. His epaulettes are of the type favored by the militia and volunteers, rather than regular army pattern.

Above: Colonel T. J. Turner, who commanded the Fifteenth Illinois Infantry, seems to have buttons from that state on his double-breasted field grade frock coat. The shoulder-straps probably have a light blue center and bear a spread eagle to indicate his rank. His McDowell-type forage cap bears an embroidered trumpet of the type worn by officers of the Mounted Rifles, a U.S. Army regiment established during the Mexican War and redesignated the Third U.S. Cavalry in 1863.

Above: The sloping visor version of the forage cap, often referred to as the 'McDowell' pattern, is held by at least three of the officers of the Twentieth Massachusetts Volunteer Infantry's regimental staff, in 1861. The spread eagles of the regiment's colonel are evident in the center of his shoulder-straps (seated man with hand on the table).

Below: Officers of the First Connecticut Artillery at Yorktown, Virginia, in 1862, all wear nine-button single-breasted company grade frock coats and scarlet-backed shoulder-straps, with the exception of the man who appears third from the left, who has chosen what appears to be a long sack coat or jacket with five buttons. Forage caps and civilian-style slouch hats are evident, as are two oil cloth covers for forage caps on the young man standing in the rear center, and the standing officer second from the left.

Opposite page: Seated for a portrait in 1862, Captain Samuel Doten, Twenty-ninth Massachusetts Volunteer Infantry, has obtained large-sized shoulder-straps with double bars at each end to display his rank. His tall forage cap has a gold embroidered infantry bugle device with a silver embroidered '29.' The coat and trousers are of dark blue wool. The sword knot hanging from his M1850 foot officer's sword is gold bullion.

Above: First Lieutenant Levi Scofield has been detailed from the 103rd Ohio Volunteer Infantry to duty as a topographical engineer. Consequently he has added a shield and wreath to his cap, similar to that prescribed for topogs in the U.S. Army, and likewise Old English script letters 'T E' appear in the centers of his shoulder-straps, being placed between the gold bar at each end of the strap, the latter element being the rank symbol for first lieutenants.

Above: Captain Samuel Walden of the Thirty-third New Jersey Volunteer Infantry ('2nd Zouaves') is wearing a standard blue nine-button company grade frock coat and an embroidered wreath with the regimental numeral on his cap, which also has additional blue and red trim in keeping with those worn by the enlisted men.

Above: Captain Lewis Fassett, Sixty-fourth New York Volunteer Infantry, has opted to replace the long frock coat – often worn by officers – by a jacket that reaches slightly below the belt. The buckle on his saber belt probably bears the letters 'N.Y.' in a wreath.

Above: The U.S. Military Academy summer full dress consisted of coatee of cadet gray with ball buttons and black silk cord trim, with white duck trousers and the 1853-pattern black cap with leather top. West Pointers anxiously awaited the day that they could put aside this uniform for one of a commissioned officer.

Right: In 1861, this private of the Second Vermont Infantry turns out in gray 'doeskin' coat with buttons bearing the state seal, and trousers of the same material. They were manufactured by Merrill & Co., of Reading, Vermont. The cap was also gray, and all three items were piped in blue cord. As it turned out, the color tended toward brown rather than gray.

Left: A plain dark blue frock coat and dark blue trousers, with a 'furlough cap' that bore the embroidered letters 'U.S.M.A.' in a wreath, were authorized for cadets at West Point when they were on leave. It is possible that some graduates converted this uniform after they had graduated and received their commissions, the pattern of the frock coat being of the type worn by regular army company grade officers.

Left: The Fourth Wisconsin Infantry began the war with a gray cap, trousers, and jacket, the latter item being trimmed in black on the shoulder loops and cuff flashes. Most of the regiments from this state followed a similar course, during the first year of the conflict at least.

Opposite page: Inspired by the Seventh New York black-trimmed uniforms of gray cloth with black-and-white epaulettes and a black cap surmounted by a white pompon, was the dress kit for the Second Regiment of Massachusetts Volunteer Militia, when the war began in 1861.

Left: These soldiers of Tenth Massachusetts Volunteer Infantry hold the 1853 Enfield rifle. Imported from England, some 500,00 were purchased between 1861 (when this picture was taken and the end of 1863. The four-button sack coat prevails as do 'mud-colored' slouch hats (so described in the regimental history).

Above: In this 1861 picture Private Minor Milliman, Company 'E', Thirty-ninth Illinois Volunteer Infantry, has added a sash and sword to set off his blue cap, trousers, and jacket, the first two items not forming part of the issue, although his U.S.-converted musket was.

Above: As indicated by their name, the Philadelphia Gray Reserves had a fatigue uniform in that color, with black cuffs and flashes on the collar, seen here worn by a private of that unit in 1861.

Right: Another Philadelphia unit of 1861, the 'Caldwalader's Grays,' a company of the First Regiment Pennsylvania Artillery, wore the tall black shako which seems to have a black pompon. The trim on the uniform is probably black with gold laced overlays. Although this man is a private, the shoulder scales are of the pattern issued to NCOs in the U.S. Army beginning in the 1850s.

Above: Another example of the dandy dress favored by militiamen at the outbreak of the Civil War is evident in this picture of a member of the two-company First Corps of Cadets, Boston, 1861. This man, in his red-trimmed gray uniform and ungainly chapeau, belonged to the First Company.

Above right: Connecticut's Revolutionary War heritage is reflected by a private of the Putnam Phalanx, a quasi-military unit formed in 1858 (photographed in 1861). A black cocked hat with gilt trim and red over black feathers tops off a blue coat with buff facings, buff waistcoat, black breeches, and gilt buttons and epaulettes. A forage cap,

similar to the U.S. Army's 1839-pattern, is on the table next to this anachronistic warrior who probably never left the parade ground, at least in this kit, to fight against the Confederacy.

Opposite page: In stark contrast to such pomp, an unidentified infantry volunteer from Maine exhibits a no-nonsense Yankee outfit, which may be of gray cloth, this shade being adopted for the first six regiments raised by the state for the war. The brass belt plate, although reversed in the original image, bears the common 'V.M.M.' (Volunteer Militia Maine)

Opposite page, left: Each company of the Fifth Massachusetts Volunteer Militia had its own distinctive uniform when the Civil War erupted. Depicted here is a private of that regiment in about 1861. His gray cloth triple-breasted coat and gray trousers are probably trimmed in black or red, both colors registering about the same in photographs of the period.

Opposite page, right: Three enormous light blue worsted stripes worn points down on each sleeve above the elbow mark Charles Vickery as a sergeant. He was appointed to this rank in the Second New Hampshire Volunteer Infantry on 28 May 1862, by which time he seems to have abandoned the gray with red trimmed coatee and gray trousers in which the regiment entered federal service.

Right: Colonel Ambrose Burnside, a tailor in civilian life who later rose to be major general of volunteers, designed the First Rhode Island Detached Militia's uniform, seen here worn by a private of that unit. The brimmed hat was similar to the U.S. Army's 1858-pattern and was looped up on the left side. A loose blue blouse or shirt of merino or heavy flannel and gray trousers constituted the simple but effective outfit.

Opposite page: The Forty-second Pennsylvania Volunteer Infantry (also referred to variously as the Thirteenth Regiment Pennsylvania Reserves, the First Rifle Regiment, and Kanes Rifles) gained yet another name, 'Bucktails', because of the deer tail or deer hide badge which the unit wore on its caps. This sergeant, as indicated by his worsted chevrons on the sleeve of a coat which appears to be little more than a civilian sack with military buttons and insignia added, is wearing blue trousers with dark blue worsted 1½-inch leg stripes. He has a blue V Corps Third Division badge on the front of his bummer's cap.

Above: Beginning in the summer of 1863, with the Third Division of III Corps, cloth or metallic devices gradually

began to be adopted to distinguish major units from one another. For example, Sergeant Michael Lawn of the Ninety-fifth Pennsylvania Volunteer Infantry ('Gosline's Zouaves') displays his VI Corps badge (a Greek Cross) on the top of his forage cap.

Above: In late summer 1862 the 149th and 150th Regiments of Pennsylvania Volunteers were created and likewise placed deer tails in their caps, although the men of the old Thirteenth reacted by calling the newcomers 'Bogus Bucktails'. Both units would have the chance to show their valor and earn the nickname at such engagements as Gettysburg. This private is probably from the 150th PV.

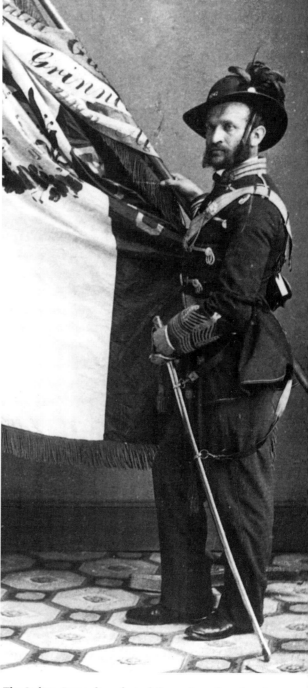

Above: Ethnic and national origins were sometimes evident in certain units. This sergeant of the Seventy-ninth New York State Militia wears his glengarry at a rakish angle in emulation of Highland fashion inspired by 'the old gallant 42nd Scots', according to a November 1858 article describing the unit when consideration was being given to its formation in that year. The jackets were blue with red facings; the men often came from Scotland or were of Scottish ancestry.

Above right: There is no doubt about the origins of the outfit worn by the Thirty-ninth Volunteer Infantry; the unit was known among other names as the 'Garibaldi Guard'.

The Italian *Bersagliere* hat of the regiment's colonel, Frederick G. d'Utassy, and his surname tell the story. The coat for officers was dark blue with gold frogging on the breast and gold lace on the sleeves. The men had red trim on their coats.

Opposite page: The Eighty-eighth New York Volunteers formed part of the 'Irish Brigade', where they were known as the Fifth Regiment, or by their nickname, 'Meaher's Own'. This first sergeant, with the chevrons of that rank prominently displayed, holds the regiment's banner with yellow Irish harp.

pposite page: Other militiamen preferred rench martial attire, even if slightly outdated, s seen here with these two men from an nidentified San Francisco unit of about 1861, ith their tail coats, sometimes known as lawhammer' or 'swallowtails'. The cap with igh pompon is based on a pre-1860 French tyle.

ight: Colonel Philippe Regis Denis de Keredern e Trobriand, true to his French origins, ommanded 'La Garde Lafayette', six companies f which had a French-style uniform, including gray-blue overcoat lined and trimmed in red, red forage cap with blue band, and red rousers. But not only those of French heritage ere enamored of Gallic martial attire.

elow: In the 1830s the French Zouaves were ormed from a tribe of Berber warriors known s *Zouaoua*. In time these troops in their istinctly North African dress achieved onsiderable fame, and gave rise to imitators in he United States. Various militia units adapted he Zouave kit in many ways, the most common eing a short jacket with lace loosely based on he *tombeau*, or twining lace which formed the op and cloverleaf on either side of the outer arment worn by the French Army Zouaves r *Tirailleurs Algériéns* (Turcos). Among the mitators were the Duryee's Zouaves (Fifth New ork Volunteer Infantry) seen here at Fort Monroe, Virginia, in 1861.

Opposite page, top: Company 'A' of the Eighth Regiment of Massachusetts Volunteer Infantry, known as the 'Salem Zouaves' retained the gray overcoat issued by the state, but wore a blue jacket, vest, and baggy trousers trimmed in red. The company wore red forage caps, but three of the officers, standing in front, have donned a pseudo fez. The men had been detailed to serve as a guard for U.S.S. *Constitution* when it was deemed prudent to sail her from Annapolis, Maryland, to New York harbor to prevent her capture.

Opposite page, bottom left: Although the other ranks of the Thirty-third New Jersey Volunteer Infantry adopted zouave dress, their officers, such as First Lieutenant William Lambert, purchased standard frock coats that were modified to feature special trim on the cuffs. Officers' forage caps also had braid, although Lambert evidently found a slouch hat more to his liking.

Opposite page, bottom right: A more directly adopted French garment was the *chasseur* uniform, which was actually imported from France to be issued to such State units as the Eighty-third Pennsylvania Volunteer Infantry. They are represented here by a private in the blue 1860-pattern *Chasseur de Vincennes* jacket with yellow worsted epaulettes, medium blue baggy pants with yellowish gaiters, some of which were leather and others linen, white leggings, and a black leather cap with black cock feathers. The uniform lasted only until March 1862.

Right: The Fourth Battalion Massachusetts Volunteer Militia (New England Guards) adopted a uniform after the fashion of the French *chasseurs*, with kepi, gaiters, and knots on the shoulders. The jacket was blue. The outfit was made in the United States, rather than being imported.

Opposite page: Three stripes worn above the elbow points down and three tie bars across the top were the rank insignia of regimental quarter-master sergeants. This example is shown by D. B. Fleming of the Twelfth West Virginia Infantry. Being an infantry unit, the color was to be light blue, and the material, if it followed U.S. Army regulation, was to be silk, rather than worsted which was prescribed for corporals, sergeants, and orderly or first sergeants.

Right: The sky-blue kersey overcoat adopted for enlisted foot troops in 1851, and which continued as a common item of issue for more than a decade, had a short cape which was attached to the single-breasted garment that fastened with five buttons. The cap is of the *chasseur* style for this unidentified private.

Above: In 1851 the U.S. Army adopted a handsome cloak coat for officers based on the French Army's *capote*. The dark blue overcoat could be worn with or without cape. Black silk braid galloons indicated rank, as in the case of Dewitt Baker, Seventy-second Pennsylvania Volunteer Infantry ('Baker's Fire Zouaves'), where five strands grace the cuffs to designate him as the regiment's colonel.

Above right: Captain H. H. Burnett of the Fifth New York Volunteer Infantry wore a coat similar to the 1851-pattern with galloons on each cuff to indicate his rank, but instead of the coat fastening with frogs, gilt buttons were used.

Opposite page: Officers frequently availed themselves of the option of wearing an enlisted overcoat. Lieutenant Albion Dudley, Fifty-eighth Massachusetts Volunteer Infantry, appears to have obtained a standard 1851-pattern enlisted overcoat for mounted troops, which has a pocket added on the right, and a cape lined perhaps in dark blue. The collar of his single-breasted dark blue woollen frock coat shows slightly above the overcoat in this 1864 picture.

Left: Two regiments of sharpshooters were raised in 1861. This unidentified private from the Second Regiment U.S. Sharpshooters, carries the Colt revolving rifle, and is wearing the distinctive frock coat and cap, both of green cloth, which was the trademark of the two units. A black ostrich feather is fastened to the front of his cap. The trousers are sky-blue and the trim on the coat emerald green. A gray woollen 'seamless' overcoat, also with green trim, is rolled on his Prussian-style knapsack and held by straps at the top.

Above: The 1858-pattern dark blue single-breasted frock coat, piped in sky-blue for infantrymen, saw considerable use in camp and on campaign, being issued to regulars and some volunteers alike. The 1858-pattern hat, looped on the left side for foot soldiers as per the regulations, was to bear a brass hunting-horn and company letters, together with the regimental number, although the latter insignia is absent. The chevrons are light blue worsted tape to match the piping on this sergeant's coat. A 1½-inch dark blue leg stripe is sewn to the outer seams of the sky-blue kersey

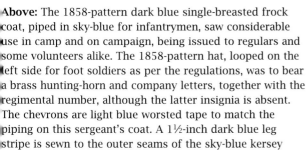

trousers. A black, shoe leather belt adopted for use with the M1855 rifle is likewise evident with its attached frog and sword bayonet in the brass tipped and throated leather scabbard.

Above: The 1858-pattern hat was not as popular as the forage cap, here being worn by a private of the Forty-fourth Massachusetts Volunteer Infantry with his interlocking 'snake' buckle.

Left: Private Louis Troutman, one of more than 180,000 African Americans who joined the Union forces, was a member of the 108th U.S. Colored Volunteers. The 1858-pattern frock coat with light blue piping, sky-blue trousers, and plain forage cap was the standard dress for this unit.

Right: An unidentified
sergeant with the
regimental standard
of the 108th U.S.
Colored Volunteer
Infantry is wearing the
special belt used by a
color-bearer. The light
blue trim of his
uniform coat, the
chevrons, and the 1½-
inch worsted leg
stripe have been hand
tinted.

Opposite page: Infantry and heavy artillery musicians wore the same single-breasted nine-button frock coats as line troops except for a special lace trim which can be seen here on this infantry drummer. The young man's coat is too large, so the cuffs have been rolled up, thereby obscuring some of the light blue piping on what otherwise is a representative image of the 1861–5 era. He also has the M1840 musician's sword held by an over-the-shoulder sling with its attached circular brass eagle plate.

Above: It is possible that this trooper is a member of Company 'C', First United States Cavalry, given that all the uniform elements, including the 1854-pattern mounted

jacket with yellow lace trim and shoulder scales of a private, and the 1858-pattern hat, appear to be of regular army issue. A leather saber knot hangs from the hilt of his M1859 light cavalry saber, and an over-the-shoulder strap supports his black leather saber belt.

Above: Another private, perhaps of the Sixth Cavalry, formed in 1863, appears in the dress uniform set forth in the 1861 regulations, including the mounted troops' sky-blue kersey reinforced trousers. The seam of the reinforcement is particularly noticeable on the inner right leg.

Above: Colonel Louis di Cesnola was commanding the Fourth New York Volunteer Cavalry when he had this picture taken in about 1862. This officer, who was destined to receive the Medal of Honor, is wearing a French-style kepi which bears the crossed sabers and '4'; his double-breasted jacket was of the type favored by field grade officers of mounted units as early as the 1840s. The overcoat appears to be light blue with five strands of black braid to indicate rank. The colonel has slung a pelisse over his right shoulder.

Above right: Although the Sixth Pennsylvania Volunteer Cavalry was officially designated the Seventieth Volunteers, the unit's most popular name was 'Rush's Lancers' because of the fact the troops were authorized to carry a 9-foot long lance with an 11-inch triple-edged blade. The commander

was Colonel Charles H. Rush, seen here with a patented cavalry cap-hat. This had not only a visor, but flaps on the sides which could be turned to form a brim. Rush is wearing a standard field grade officer's frock coat and has tied his crimson silk sash on the left side, contrary to U.S. Army regulation.

Opposite page: The Fifth Pennsylvania Volunteer Cavalry carried both Colt Army .44 caliber revolvers, as seen here, and .36 caliber Whitney Navy revolvers. The black slouch hat bears inverted 1858-pattern U.S. cavalry and dragoon brass sabers insignia with the regimental numeral above and company letter below as well as a 'P' and a 'V' in brass for Pennsylvania Volunteers. The jacket is patterned after the U.S. Army model, but it appears that the lace on the collar is in single rather than double rows.

Above: Louis Fagan was a member of the Anderson Troop, an independent company of volunteer cavalry called to arms in October 1861 at Carlisle, Pennsylvania, and named in honor of the commander of Fort Sumter. Eventually an entire regiment was raised and designated the Fifteenth Pennsylvania ('Anderson') Cavalry. Also nicknamed 'Rosy's Ponies', when they were assigned to the Army of Ohio under William S. Rosecrans, the troop remained active until 1863. The patented cavalry cap-hat was a hallmark of the unit, with crossed 1851-pattern dragoon officer's-type metallic saber insignia mounted on the front. The jacket is a variation of the U.S. Army's 1854-pattern with extra seams flanking the front buttons. Brass shoulder scales are another feature.

Above: The Third New Jersey Volunteer Cavalry Regiment (First U.S. Hussars) was formed in 1864, and because of its ornate blue uniform, made by a Newark firm, they were dubbed the 'butterflies'. This uniform was modelled on that of an Austrian hussar unit, the dark blue jacket having a 'profusion of yellow cords across the breast and on the front of the collar an orange colored ground'. Ball buttons were sewn on in three rows. This first sergeant, as indicated by the chevrons with the lozenge above, has crossed sabers insignia on his cap with the numeral '3' of the regiment displayed.

Right: Bands formed an integral part of many units and had great latitude in the style of their uniforms, such as this unidentified musician of the Fourteenth New York State Militia.

Left: The drum major of the Fifth New York State Militia sported chevrons similar to a sergeant major, but had the additional device of a star in the center. He also wore services stripes above his cuff flashes, after the fashion of the regulars, and adorned his plastron front triple-breasted coat with officer's epaulettes. He carries a baton and has slung a baldric over his right shoulder as further accessories to his ornate outfit.

Opposite page, top: The band of the Twelfth Indiana Volunteer Infantry wore the same quasi-zouave uniforms as the infantrymen of that regiment. Many other Department of the Gulf units wore similar uniforms made to look like vested zouave jackets.

Opposite page, bottom left: First Lieutenant David Hamel of the Sixth Regiment, New York Heavy Artillery, wears a single galloon on each cuff of his jacket as well as shoulder-straps with a single gold bar at each end on a scarlet field to indicate his rank. Gold embroidered crossed cannon insignia are sewn to the front of his forage cap with a '6' in the center where the artillery pieces intersect.

Opposite page, bottom right: The brass 'turnkey' and bar or staple that held the shoulder scales in place are evident on the nine-button 1858-pattern frock coat worn by Private Fritz Egistrom, Company 'A', First Battalion, Massachusetts Heavy Artillery. So too is the leather neck stock which was not a popular item among the rank and file who called it a 'dog collar' or other derisive terms.

Opposite page, left:
The light artillery cap with scarlet worsted cords and matching horsetail plume was issued to some regular army and volunteer horse artillery units alike, as seen here in his *circa* 1865 portrait of a private. The jacket has a slightly more rounded edge and shorter collar than the pattern adopted by the U.S. Army in 1854.

Opposite page, right:
Another light artillery private appears in a similar pattern jacket with shoulder scales, and the forage cap bearing the 1858-pattern crossed cannon insignia prescribed for the dress hat or cap. The reinforcing on the inner legs of the trousers is evident.

Right: Heavy artillery-men, such as this member of the Third Pennsylvania, in 1864, often wore the single-breasted nine-button enlisted frock coat with scarlet piping or trim on the collar and cuffs. The man's headgear is either an 1858-pattern regulation hat which has been creased fore and aft, or a similar black civilian hat with the scarlet cord and brass insignia affixed.

Above: During the siege of Charleston, South Carolina, a pair of Union Parrott cannon located in Battery Meade, Morris Island, prepare to go into action in August 1863. Most of the heavy or siege artillerymen are wearing four-button sack coats, one of the most common outer garments by the mid to late war, Also, they are wearing forage caps, with the notable exception of the gunner in the striped shirt. His nondescript hat was perhaps sent from home or purchased from a local sutler as being more suitable for the hot, humid climate.

Below: Company 'I', Tenth Regiment Veteran Reserve Corps standing at ease, Washington, DC, 1865, the final year of the war. By this time the dark blue bummer's cap, four-button sack, and sky-blue kersey trousers were issued extensively to Union infantry and many other branches, the diverse array of federal uniforms extant at the opening of the conflict now only a memory. The North's industrial capabilities made it possible to achieve this state of uniformity for a large army, reaching at its peak strength upwards of a million men.

INDEX